SEVEN
YEAR
SILENCE

SEVEN
YEAR
SILENCE

poems by

Taya Sanderson Kesslau

ROOTS PRESS
ESTD 2023

ROOTS PRESS
ESTD 2023

ISBN 979-8-9889532-0-3
Library of Congress Control Number: pending

Cover art and design by Megan Ball
Typesetting by Enterline Design Services

Printed in the United States of America

Published by Roots Press, LLC
Bellingham, Washington
tayawholehearted@gmail.com
rootspressprinting.com

for taya gray

you were braver than you knew. thank you for delivering us into the wide open spaces of love~

CONTENTS

PREFACE

Seven Year Silence is a collection of poems I wrote during my long journey through divorce. This is also a book about death, grief, loss. Fear, hope, disappointment. Listening and discovery.

During the unraveling of my marriage, a new voice rose up out of me. The voice of poetry. Through the darkest depths of that journey, the poems I wrote became points of light to me. Shining clarity and illuminating a new path. Eventually, I no longer fit into the tight, restrictive spaces that once held me.

As the dust of my divorce was settling and I found myself writing less, I had a sense that the poetry I had written needed a space to rest. I thought it might be many years before I would be able to share it, if at all, and felt that my own healing was a process best accomplished in quiet anonymity. So, I created a file and called it Seven Year Silence.

My divorce was final in January 2015. Seven years have passed and then some. It's time for the silence to end. Those poems that came to me as gifts through that desperate and difficult time in my life, have grown little wings during their time of rest and healing. They are ready to make their way into the world. Into the hearts of others who may be in the depths of their own grief or despair. Candles of warmth and light to hopefully guide other broken souls into a harbor of kindness and rest.

If you have known grief or walked in darkness, if you have loved and lost, if you crave honesty, healing, hope and light, these poems are for you~

~T

PART I

UNBECOMING
ONENESS

Resilience

I am free. This is true.
You may not know it
since I am your wife.

I am young.
The beauty of my youth lingers.
Resilience too.

I even listen well
to your endless critiques
against me.

But let me remind you
I am free.
And though I tarry in Egypt
as I am bound to

there is a fierce wind blowing.
And I've heard the seas are
drying.

Regardless
I am a strong swimmer.

Mercy

Oh, that I could melt
into the rain. Washed.
Washing.

Those sanctifying droplets
that feed the Earth.

How good She is
to breathe them
back up

to grateful clouds
who cry and cry
for us all.

My House

This beautiful old house
so filled with life and character.
The years have caused the glass to run.
From room to room to room
cracks in nearly all the weeping panes.

Not so unlike me
as I dare to look
outside myself.
Every view is marred.

Broken lines
betray the truth.
My fear.
The years.

The inevitable pull of gravity.
That falling, fractured flow
which marks us all
who live here.

Chaos

My boy perches at the edge of his city
    folded in three
       a small breathing Z.
He plays with a shriveled red balloon
    chaos behind him
       and me behind that.

The Game of Marriage Counseling

So many moving pieces.
The boot. The wheelbarrow.
That top hat.
Even the cards and money
for play, trade, negotiations.

The board laid out between us.
Al in his chair, neutral.
The game begins.
No one here is neutral.

Even the money isn't real.
Still, these pieces were treasures to me
as a child.
I see how it is now though.
Trinkets. Pawns

the way you handle them
carelessly.
The way you handle me
carelessly.

And there can only be one winner.
I move. You move.
Al, in his chair, neutral.
The board laid out
between us.

This round it's you.
You say it's me. It's not
it's you. Your move.
The manipulation. The one winner.

There isn't redemption
here for me.
Not in the cards. Not even a chance.
There's no dice
that gives me advantage.

Around the board we go. Around
we go. And again. You collecting.
You gaining. Us losing.
Al in his chair, neutral.

This board laid out between us.
A session. A round completed.
You hand over some money
to Al, in his chair,
neutral.

Below

Below the depths of me
the wounds in various stages of healing
my attempts at wellness
stretch row upon row of shallow graves.

Piles of dirt betray the horrors.
Rising corpses sneer
You thought I was dead...

In that wrecked debris
lingers the aroma of Eden.

But which is worse
the dying
or the rising?

Watch me

I say as I give
my finger
to the universe.

Watch me live as a stone
and not be hurt
or bruised
or sick with love.

Beyond just me and him.
Me – cold and small.
Him– a tremendous sucking vacuum
pulling the stars down
one by one.

Watch me walk through
this world alone
in my sneakers.
Shining, damn it.
Bleeding with life.

Flightless Bird

I once rode across
a continent on the back
of a horse.
That night in the moonlight
I swam in the shallows.

Such fine young men
growing under this roof.
Under my wings

clipped to keep me still now.
Me, a flightless bird now.
Sick with the earth.
Sick with gravity.

I stay.
At the heart of me
are my sons.

At the heart of me I stand perched to fly
off the bow of a sailing ship
anchored off the coast
drifting lazily in a sapphire sea.

What of love

When was the day
I woke to find myself within
this sticky, swallowing darkness?
Though I move through it
there is never progress
and seldom light.

Tentative steps betray my suspicion
as I roam through this nightmare
hands out before me hoping
groping.

There is the hand that grabs back.
Claws me toward its need.
Also another. A glad knowing touch.
Up the length of that arm
I know the kind smile
though I cannot see it for the darkness.

No question
which way I veer
in this dark space.
No question at all.

And yet the holy institution
damns me to the clawing.
What of love, I wonder?
What of god.

Simplicity

It's selfishness, I know.
And yet there it is again,
death, my only hope.

The only release from my vow.
The only release that is
not complicating.

Imagine that,
death
not complicating.

That Next Place

This is all so familiar.
The coffee shop
chosen at random.
Me in the corner
hiding. Hurt.
Will it ever end?

A message from Mom
How are things?
Same. I'm afraid
it will never end.
My brokenness.
My inability to see him
for who he really is.

And worse
my moments of levity
and happiness when
he is gone.

For always
there is the coming back.

All That.

My heart is sick.
The old Indian has spoken to me
in my dreams.
Fear itself is a season.
Holding hands with him is death.

What's left for me to say
in this season of death.
I'm stone. I'm sunk.
From below I look
up.

Solitude consumes me
and fire too from somewhere deep.
Passionate, burning,
I sink some more.

A thousand times I've
swallowed the sea.
Drowning. Drowned.
Burning.

The tormenters have their way
with me.
Fear, despair. I am
ravaged. Burned.

Voices sing to me
in my dreams.
Fear itself is a season.
Holding hands with him is death.

The optimists and saints
glory in the new beginnings.
Life after death. Redemption and
all that.

For me, though.
For the stone.
Life after life?
What for me?

My heart is sick.
My hope deferred.
The old Indian has spoken to me
in my dreams.
Fear itself is a season.
Holding hands with him is death.

Dinnertime

The table is set.
Everyone in place.
Sustenance too.
Me too.

And then the waves rise.
Anxiety, looming
tidal wave style. That wall
of water building momentum.
The inevitable crash. My crash.

The dishes are cleared.
The family cleared.
Until tomorrow evening.

The Valley Of The Shadow

Psalm 23 for the realist

The Lord is my shepherd
I shall know grief.
He makes me lie down.
He leads me beside.

The restoring of my soul
on hold. My soul the stone
thick in my chest.
Swollen with sorrow.

I walk through the valley
of the shadow of death
where I shall know grief.
I know grief.

And speaking of death
this thing is not dead.
It lives and struggles to live
like all living things at their end.

In the valley. In the shadow.
Death.

New Mercies

I find myself once again
carelessly foraging through
my neatly ordered books.
Mary Oliver. Wendell Berry. Tolkien.
Donne. The usual suspects.

Hoping for comfort
somewhere.
Consolation. Meaning.

What I really want
to do is vomit.
To purge and cry.
And cry.

A lot of good that
will do. This always ends
the same way.

I tell myself
it doesn't matter.
What I want doesn't matter.

What I think
is important
isn't important.

Then I'll force air
into these shallow lungs.
Swallow it all down
and strain into tomorrow.

Rumor has it
there are new
mercies there.

Monday, though

Chaos will walk through my
front door. It will strip
my authority. It will sleep
in my bed. It will rob me and
then it will tell me it loves me
and leave me a hollowed-out ruin.

Greening

I saw a cicada in the summer grass
struggle from his dried
brown skin. From a
crack down the center he
entered the world bright green
and glossy moist with life.

It made me ponder where
I am in my own cycle of
life. For all the living I
hope I have in me.

He came out perfect,
except for the little
nubs I mistook for
malformed legs.

There is plenty
deformed in me.
Oh for a chance
to be green again.

And then those awkward
stubs uncurled
into wings of the most
magnificent and fragile sort.

If only I could unfurl.
Already I am split down
the center. Me with the
crippled nubs, the dying
and the striving. So much lost.

There was some stumbling
and then he flew!

The Other Side

Through my
weariness
I peered across

the chasm. The
skies were blue
with wisps of white.

The earth was
green and gold. Did
I detect ease

and gladness, joy
and gratitude?
What was it

the cicadas were
buzzing as I jealously
followed shadows of

frogs beneath
the murky
water?

I came
so
close.

Even the darkness
of the shade
was delicious.

Unbecoming

We, as the children of
God, are becoming new.
All that good truth
in church for everyone

but me.

I find myself unbecoming.

Unbecoming oneness.

Lean into the sharp points
the Buddhists say.
Know the process.
Be in the process.

The unbecoming process.

Unbecoming

me.

A Question

What makes us think
we are meant to be happy?

With the curse of sin,
sweat. Heartache.
The pain of being bettered – battered.

I nod in agreement
to avoid endless conflict.
What I want is to be happy.
To rest in ease and work and commune.

To love and be held
in love. Maybe even cherished.

For someone to say,
I just used a hand soap that
reminded me of the way your
hair smelled today.

Plea.

Echoes of vigor
perishing. Starving,
you partake of the feast
that is me. I sup along
with you out of duty.
All these years just me
and you. Only you.
And yet now out of the depths
of me there is a new voice.
Mine. A comforting cry.
It pleads for another chance
at life. At love.
For the slave to be free
of the feasting. Because
I am starving too.

PART II

·····························

MEXICO –
THE COUNTDOWN

Mexico

Seabirds of magnificent feature
soar high above
eternal ebbing and flooding.

I am here to learn that too
graceful soaring high above.

This whole wide ocean
sends its waves
two by two

to crash upon the waiting sand.
Another element I am here
to learn about.

On The Beach After Dinner In Mexico

Why did you bring me down here
to walk on the beach then?
You demand on the beach after dinner.
The sky is lit with the most
lovely hue of purple.

I am puzzled
since we walk on the beach
every night after dinner.
I thought we did it for the beauty,
the company we keep.
As part of our adventure here
in Mexico.

I see my error now.
I should not be beautiful.
As your wife I owe you my body.
You have taught me this
from the beginning.

My beauty is my sentence.
You take what you want.
Choice is never mine
with you. Even in Mexico.

Purple Stones

Purple stones dot the sand
alongside the carcasses of clams
and abalone.
Their iridescent remains reflecting
light up to me
in a thousand colors
I have never seen.
So much beauty
in this death.

This Room, Alone.

I am so tired of being bettered.
He is endlessly sad
and regardless of the diplomacy
it is always my fault.

Meanwhile the mariachi band.
Meanwhile the students of Mexico
intertwine limbs and move together like
the fins of fish.

Meanwhile the fireworks
of some celebration
flash and smoke out
over the ocean.

I sit here in this room alone.
This luxurious third world room.
No tears left. No more surrendering.
The countdown has begun.

The Third World

There is a phantom
mystique
to third world countries.

An unpredictable beauty
deep and hidden slyly
beneath their poverties.

Where you are afraid
I am enticed.

A seductive specter calls to me
Come down this shabby path.
Up the hillside I follow
expectantly.

Beyond the bashful lizards.
Up. Up to the highest lighthouse
in the world. Well, second highest,
but who is counting?

And there I stand
the specter and I – breathless.
Full of wonder.
Full of life.

And what did I learn there?
That your poverty calls to fear
and he is a dominating force
over my spectral beauty.

Fear will not be told to go
or to stay for that matter, either.
But makes himself
at home on this peak
down in the city
in your heart
in the space between us.

And now I know what
keeps men from beauty.
What keeps you.

We are a predictable pair down here
me and my beautiful phantom
you and your poverty.

There is no need
for us to come
here again.

Clouds

A skeletal hand in the Mexican sky.
How fitting.
Seabirds weaving in and out
of wispy finger bones.
Maybe it's just the tequila.

You feel it too.
Tears in your eyes and in your mouth
You don't love me, I know it.
I listen soberly and feel very sad
for you.

You continue.
And yet I am distracted
by two terns playfully rolling
near the thumb.
They are drawn in orbit around
one another

and I see myself in another lifetime
with another.

So I do not wish
to be plucked by that great hand
but left to tarry here
until my time comes to fly.

Though Hope

Emerald crests lift and roll.
A violent sucking undertow.
I know it well.
Glorious if I have breath to spare.
Terror if not.

I am accustomed to both
the weightless youthful lifting
the pulling pulling -
You will not make it this time.

Nothing is for certain
though hope floats
my gaze upward
beyond those emerald crests
toward a new horizon.

For Beauty

In the end
what has Mexico taught me?
Beauty.

I can withstand one hundred hours and more
of your cursing and crying out
if only
for beauty.

I can stand naked and accused
and even admit you are right,
I do not love you well,
if in the end
a beautiful story can be told.

I can tarry in Egypt
as a slave
if on the last page
beauty gets to win.

In this third world country
of death and poverty and fear,
of coupled gliding seabirds
and lavender horizons.

Wave upon emerald wave of
purple stones and shells radiating
thousands of glowing hues.

If I can believe them in the end
maybe it will be worth it after all.
Maybe I can ride boldly back into the
battles of my life with
a shining standard over me -
For beauty.

PART III

THESE DAYS

These Days

These days I like to be out
in the world. All those years
tied down, I allowed it.

I wanted to fly. You told me
no. Wait until the children are
grown. Same thing as no.

From my new perspective on
the peak, in the field, by the lake,
not even the sky is my limit.

Acknowledgements

Many people were instrumental in bringing Seven Year Silence to publication. I want to thank Gail Noble-Sanderson, my mentor and my second mother. She blazed a trail into all things self-publishing, and I have benefitted greatly from her courage and resourcefulness. Linda Conroy, my unofficial and very generous editor. To my community of poets, these dear people have been a wonderful sounding board for me as I tweaked and re-tweaked these poems. Their honesty and creativity have made this work better. My friend and artistic-tech expert, Megan, for all things front and back cover. To Jason Enterline for expertise and expediency in type-setting and publishing advisements. Special thanks to my Women – all of them. And there are a lot, (living and dead), who have contributed life and love and solidarity to me. Who have modeled fierceness and tenderness and flexibililty and growth. They taught me to stand and their love helped me bloom; to my Mom for teaching me to keep my eyes open, and to my Dad for ever-present, deep currents of love and wisdom; Lauren, my best friend in the world. Her voice is the voice in my head that quiets the mean girls.

And finally, I want to thank my new husband, Greg, for teaching me to be a happy human. We do get to do what we want, my love!